The Stones of the Parthenon

Manolis Korres

The Stones of the Parthenon

MELISSA Publishing House

This book is based on the first part
of *From Pentelicon to the Parthenon*,
published by Melissa Publishing House in 1995.

First English edition:
Text: © 2000 Melissa Publishing House, Athens
Illustrations: © 2000 Manolis Korres

Dr. D. Turner, *English Translation*
Athina Ragia, *Layout*
Kelly Tamaki, *Cover Design*

Printed and bound in Greece

Melissa Publishing House
58 Skoufa Str., 106 80 Athens, Greece
Tel.: +30 210 3611692, Fax: +30 210 3600865
www.melissabooks.com

ISBN 960 204 205 2

Contents

Most visitors to the Athenian Acropolis have wondered how the large masses of marble used for the monuments were originally hauled to the top of the sacred rock. People familiar with the ancient buildings may regard such speculation as superfluous, at times scoffing at a visitor's perplexed questions, which appear to betray a failure to appreciate the Acropolis monuments as achievements of art and of the intellect rather than as products of manual labor. But it is a mistake to assert that attention should be paid only to the purely immaterial and intellectual part of the achievement.

Nevertheless, it would appear that people who admire manual labor and those who do not all have one thing in common. They recognize only a few—and, indeed, the most easily comprehensible—of ancient architecture's technical accomplishments. They do not realize that certain stages of the work, such as quarrying and transporting the marble blocks, were much more demanding than the job of raising them into position; they are unaware that the most difficult task of all was smoothing and joining the blocks.

The technological achievements of ancient Greek craftsmen, however, did not end with the assembly of massive marble blocks. In the field of metalwork, the Greeks manufactured sophisticated stone-cutting implements. Judging from the marks they left on the marble, these tools must have been of much higher quality than their modern counterparts. Apparently, certain craftsmen in antiquity had, after much systematic experimental research, discovered unsurpassed metallurgical processes. Detailed knowledge about these processes is unavailable to us today, along with so many other secrets that were lost with the decline of the ancient world.

If they had been required to use modern-day stone-cutting implements, ancient stone masons and sculptors would have taken at least twice as long to construct the Parthenon, and the quality of the surfaces would not have approached the level of perfection left by ancient tools. In that hypothetical scenario, the building would have remained unfinished when the Peloponnesian War broke out in 431 B.C. And because the Parthenon's completion was a basic prerequisite for the construction of the gateway to the Acropolis, the Propylaea might never have been erected.

Given the unique quality of ancient stone masonry and the structural bulk of the Parthenon, it is clear that it would be impossible today to duplicate the perfectly constructed temple in the astounding time of eight years. This remains true even if we were to employ the same number of experienced craftsmen, and even if gasoline-powered vehicles replaced animal-drawn wagons, or electric cranes were used instead of manually operated ones. However strange this conclusion may sound, it is well documented.

For a building such as the Parthenon, the greatest possible demands of refinement and accuracy occur during the final stages, in the preparation of each block, of each column, of each sculpted figure. Those demands far exceed the requirements involved in the early stages of construction, when quarrying, transporting, and hoisting the blocks constitute simply one part of the process. Therefore, it has been calculated that, in the case of the Parthenon, using an ancient wooden crane instead of a modern electric one would create a disadvantage of economy of only 3 percent, while using wagons instead of gas-powered vehicles would create a disadvantage of between 10 and 20 percent. However, the ancient tools' unique metallurgical quality, combined with the stone masons' incredible technical prowess, would create an advantage over present methods and standards that quantitatively exceeds 100 percent and qualitatively remains incalculable.

Unlike many modern architects, ancient architects and sculptors did not take their tools and technologies for granted. An ancient architect was often responsible for planning the mechanical means used by his craftsmen, as well as for establishing standards of manual labor for them. A good quarryman would bear in mind the problems faced by the sculptor or the architect and would make calculations that demanded careful consideration. He had to observe, evaluate, and handle a very difficult material. He had to comprehend complex combinations of geological, geometrical, artistic, and mechanical factors. A worthy craftsman had, generally speaking, a broad range of theoretical interests and, when these combined with exceptional talent, a career as an architect was by no means impossible. Finally, all these factors had to operate within a perfectly organized system of work and production, which in itself represented an exceptional intellectual undertaking.

Unfortunately, this achievement has been almost completely ignored in modern times, for it is perceived as being neither artistic nor imbued with ideals. But why should a great project be arbitrarily divided into higher intellectual and lower manual or "managerial" components? Why should those who, in their own field, exhibited all the characteristics of a creative artist—even a minor one—be considered nothing more than ordinary laborers?

The following pages are devoted to precisely these minor but important craftsmen and to that combination of boldness and imagination manifested in the physical exertion of their bodies. Although this exertion may have taken a toll on their mortal selves, it was rewarded not simply with a day's wage but with an eternity that only the natural immortality of marble can secure.

Sadly, modern exploitation of marble at the site of the ancient quarries on Mount Pentelicon, which got under way slowly from 1834 to 1940 and reached a feverish pitch in the reconstruction period after World War II, has destroyed about 90 percent of the ancient quarries. Among the extant remains of those quarries are many—often huge—cuttings, rock faces, and pits, carefully formed dumps for chips and flakes, ancient roads, and so on. Most are situated in a continuous zone extending almost 3 kilometers along the south side of the central mass of Mount Pentelicon.

This book reconstructs the process of quarrying a block of marble for an 11-ton Doric column capital and transporting it from the Pentelicon quarry to the Acropolis at Athens, relating its adventures as they interweave themselves with those of the people and the city in general. It begins shortly after the Athenians' great victory over their archenemy, the Persians, in the Battle of Marathon, in 490 B.C.

The story of the half-finished column capital presented here fulfills a long-standing desire of mine. Therefore, I would like to thank those who encouraged me in this undertaking: D. Kalapothakis, D. Korres, M. Spyratou, K. Chatziaslani, and especially my wife, K. Korre. I also owe thanks to T. Biles and M. Magnisali for the invaluable help provided by their studies on the reconstruction of the ancient quarries and to professors Ch. Bouras and G. Gruben for the discussions on the subject they were kind enough to have with me.

Finally, I should like to take the opportunity to thank especially the director of Melissa Publications, Mr. G. Rayas, and all those with whom I was fortunate to work in an attempt to save the ancient quarries from destruction and ransacking.

M. Korres

1. Athens and Her Quarries

Only five years have elapsed since the unforgettable Battle of Marathon, in 490 B.C. Building activities are clearly visible on the Acropolis in the heart of Athens, and they can be seen from as far away as the island of Aegina. The oldest of the temples of Athena is no longer visible, for giant scaffolding has been erected around three of its sides. The Athenians are replacing the old building with a much larger temple, which, like all the temples in Athens, will be in the Doric order.

However, Doric architecture's favorite material, poros stone (hard limestone which was being quarried on the Piraeus hills), will not be used for this new structure. Instead, a material commonly used for Ionic buildings in the islands of the Cyclades and on the other side of the Aegean will be employed—marble! For the first time, marble will be used on a massive scale, in this case for the entire superstructure of a temple. Its solid base and foundations, made of very large, carefully cut marble blocks, are 80 meters long and 12 meters high. The scaffolding rises along almost the entire length of the foundation, hinting at the new temple's bulk.

Slightly to the north stands the limestone Temple of Athena, which, while visible from any location in the Attic basin, appears suddenly quite small next to the marble temple's gigantic scaffolding.[1] But there is another change in the landscape, one that is visible from every direction. About 17 kilometers northeast of the city, halfway down the side of the mountain called the Pentelicon, a massive, deep quarry grows larger by the day. Despite its size, this is a young quarry, created specifically to provide marble for the new temple.

Previously, only limited surface areas had been quarried for marble, which was used for statues and small architectural elements. Such objects do not need large quantities of marble, but they do require the highest possible quality. For this and various other reasons, marble imported from the Aegean island of Paros, in the Cyclades, had been preferred since the time of Pisistratus and his sons more than half a century earlier. Before that, marble was imported from the island of Naxos. The best marble from Mount Hymettus, just outside Athens, was also used in small quantities, again mostly during Pisistratus's time; but, despite being carefully chosen, it was always inferior to the marble from Naxos and Paros. Until now, no marble quarry had ever been as large or as deep as the one on Pentelicon, nor had any been a clearly discernible feature in the natural landscape.

The hard stone quarries in the hills of Athens, such as the famous Barathron quarry, were much bigger, and the limestone quarries on the coast near the harbor of Piraeus were bigger still. The largest structure made from limestone is the half-finished Temple of Olympian Zeus: 113 meters long, with columns 2 1/2 meters in diameter. It was the most ambitious architectural project undertaken by the state some thirty years earlier; work on it had been halted when the government changed.

Located to the east of the city, the Temple of Olympian Zeus still stands out impressively, and like the Acropolis, it is visible from afar, despite being built on low ground. Nevertheless, it remains a forgotten monument. Now the ambitions of the state are concentrated on the Acropolis. There the building surrounded by scaffolding, which is intended to honor Athena for the victory over the Persians and the salvation of the homeland, progresses rapidly. Thus, even as the lower drums (the cylindrical sections that make up a column) are being positioned, the builders begin to prepare the capitals for the tops of the columns so that they will be ready when the last drums are put into place.

2. The Pentelicon Quarry

Extraction has already reached a depth of nearly 20 meters in the middle of the large marble quarry. The deposit extends along all sides, but natural fissures, some vertical and others diagonal, break the continuity. The distances between fissures are not constant. In some places, fissures are close together, rendering the marble useless. Elsewhere they are so far apart that deep channels must be carved to separate the stone into required sizes. Although these fissures limit the sizes of the masses of extractable, usable marble, they provide natural openings that help make quarrying easier.

The marble's most important attribute involves the ease or difficulty of splitting it in a given direction. Knowing how to exploit this quality remains one of the basic "secrets" of the mason's art. Woodworkers quickly become experienced at recognizing the same phenomenon in their medium, for in wood it is easy to see the directions in which a cut can or cannot be made. In marble, however, those directions are sometimes not visible to the naked eye.

Another of the stonecutter's secrets involves knowledge of the faults hidden within the stone, such as discontinuity. The quarryman must carefully select the extractable masses of marble, not only by simply calculating the distances between fissures, but also by considering more complex criteria of quality involving the marble's resilience, purity, and responsiveness to precision workmanship.

Our experienced Athenian and foreign quarrymen are happy with the stone. Almost half of it can be quarried. Of that amount, only a third will be utilized; the rest will be sacrificed at various stages of the work. However, the quarrymen know they could never hope for a better result, for the original natural formation of the marble is, for the most part, very irregular, and the scission surfaces are difficult to identify. The same applies to all marble quarries when the demand is for masses of great size, regular shape, and highly workable texture.

The more experienced quarrymen—those who learned their craft in the Cyclades and Ionia— speak about these and many other things. Naturally, the temple's architects are aware of the same problems, and they probably visit the quarry regularly to inspect the stone and the work's progress. So far, about 4,200 cubic meters of marble have been extracted to produce about 1,400 cubic meters of material that will be utilized. At least half of this has been transported to the work site, where it either has been positioned or awaits positioning.

3. The Marble for the Column Capital

Down in the middle and deepest part of the quarry, a large mass of marble has attracted the attention of the experienced quarry foreman. For days, he has been calculating whether this potential block of marble can yield yet another capital for the temple's exterior colonnade.

The quarry foreman observes that the block is clearly divided from its parent rock. Two sides are exposed and the others are defined by natural fissures. The crack dividing the block from the vast subjacent mass of rock extends slightly, while the block's visible extremities indicate that it is quite regular. The foreman, trusting his experience and highly developed skills of observation, hopes that it will be easier to split and extract this block from its parent rock than it was for similar blocks.

4. Sockets for Wedges and Levers

After at last making a decision, the foreman gives directions to the specialist masons, and they, in turn, begin preparations for the first and most difficult task: splitting the massive block from the parent rock. The masons examine the length of the natural fissures and cracks that define the block, searching for the right places to insert wedges and large levers. Then they cut deep sockets into the rock, precisely trying to ensure that the distances between the sockets are correct and, in particular, that the surfaces to be cut will converge exactly. It takes many days to create perfectly positioned sockets.

5. Splitting the Block from the Parent Rock

Before the most difficult task—cleaving the designated block of marble—can begin, the iron wedges must be tested to ensure that they fit neatly in their sockets, where they will be sandwiched between iron splints. Then heavy iron levers capable of multiplying the applied pressure of a work team by up to thirty times are placed in position.[2]

With perfectly regulated rhythm, the quarrymen use short blows as they begin slowly pounding the wedges. At first, the wedges enter the rock without much difficulty, but then they become harder to hammer in. As each wedge is driven between the iron splints, its progress becomes almost imperceptible. Slowly but steadily, the reverberations of metal clashing upon metal rise from low, muted tones to a shrill, ear-piercing pitch. Following a short pause to inspect the depth to which the wedges have been driven, and after a few more blows are given to some, the most experienced of the quarrymen orders the next stage of the work to begin.

Now four heavy metal bars collectively weighing some four talents of iron (The talent, an ancient unit of weight, is equivalent to 26 kilograms.) swing in an arc through the air and, all together, pound the wedges. The quarrymen display admirable coordination as they continue to wield their mallets, and the regular repetition of the hammering becomes almost unbearable. The climax approaches in the struggle between man and rock. The sound of deep human breathing rivals that of the stormy hammering, while sweat covers the quarrymen's muscular bodies.

After hundreds of heavy blows from the heaviest of the mallets fall on the wedges and nearly superhuman effort applies pressure on the levers, muffled creaking noises announce to the tenacious quarrymen that the mass of marble is ready to part from the parent rock. The quarryman's trained ear recognizes changes in the sounds that emanate from the block as it begins to split away, sounds with hidden messages of great importance for the work's success. The creaking noises become clearer, lifting the quarrymen's spirits. There is less resistance now. Gradually but steadily, the fissures begin to loosen their hermetic hold, as clouds of fine dust rise with every new blow of the mallets.

Work pauses briefly, then the quarrymen resume their efforts, this time in a calmer atmosphere and with greater patience. Slowly but surely, the fissures open up, so much so that some of the wedges fall into the growing gap, whereupon wedges with a larger base take their place.

6. Preparing to Cut Away Excess Marble

As workers begin to expand the marble's fissures, they rely more and more on the large levers to pry the block away. Each time the space between the block and the parent rock increases slightly, slabs of rock are inserted to maintain a constant base for the application of force using the levers. After many hours of exhausting work, the gap, so small to begin with, has become wide enough to allow the quarrymen to stand inside it, for now the men must work behind the block.

A basic requirement for the extraction of this particular mass of marble is that the rough block be accessible from all sides before any attempt can be made to remove the superfluous upper surface. The quarry foreman knows that, in cases where a block has a great deal of excess marble, it is preferable to remove the first rough layer by cutting it away in individual pieces rather than in one section. He also knows that the pieces should be as large as possible, not only to minimize labor time but also to increase the chances that they will be suitable for carving other architectural elements. The foreman wants the excess marble to be used in the most profitable way, and thus the back of the block has to be pried free with the use of wedges on all four sides.

After carefully inspecting the surfaces on the back of the block, the foreman incises a few lines to act as markers for the next stage: cutting away superfluous material in the largest possible sections. The shape and incline of the veins in the marble appear to promise that almost the entire upper part of the block can be removed. Later on, four of the most experienced quarrymen execute this new task. For five days they prepare recesses, carve deep grooves, and cut twenty-one sockets for wedges.

The work is tiring and monotonous, but diversions are not lacking, even in the depths of the quarry. The men exchange jibes now and then and hold friendly competitions of dexterity. They make quick but frequent visits to the quarry's iron workshop to replace worn tools with repaired ones, break for their frugal meals, and briefly pause to help with jobs that demand a large group effort. Early each afternoon, a short but refreshing sleep boosts their spirits, but not before they chat about the latest events, the weather, the meaning of dreams, and much more.

Finally, everything is ready for cutting of the first large piece of excess marble. The wedges are positioned and the incessant repetitive hammering begins. The work continues with great care, for all the wedges must be packed into their splints at approximately the same rate to ensure an even distribution of applied force.

7. Removing Excess Marble

The first sections of excess marble are finally removed. Now, using wedges and grooves incised along the line where the stone is to be cut, further sections are excised. The master mason carefully calculates the position of these incisions so that the stone will yield a block that is as close in shape as possible to the final column capital. The marble must be compact, regular, and, most importantly, free of harmful fissures, internal faults, or interruptions of its crystalline texture.

As the excess marble is removed from the future column capital, the master mason must identify fissures and other natural imperfections, then skillfully adjust the direction in which cuts are made so that no imperfections appear in the final product. The mason learned a great deal about this problem from his old teacher, a truly worthy —albeit unlucky—craftsman from the islands, with whom he had worked closely for a few years at Delphi and on Delos. The mason's teacher had lost his life under circumstances that remain baffling to those who knew him, but his teaching lives on. Many a time he would say, "The best thing to do is to arrange the work at the quarry to ensure that faults appear only in the excess marble and not in the main mass." Then he would add, "If this is not possible, then the faults should appear only in the least susceptible, exposed, or stressed points of the final product. They should never appear in the exposed protrusions of the final shape."

The master mason calmly examines the fragments. He is almost certain that they can be used in some capacity, thanks to their size, their geological texture, and their quality. He thinks that the fragment to the right of the block could be used for a section of the east pediment cornice of the temple, and that the piece to the left would suffice, if carefully fashioned, for the production of two large *sima* tiles.

With great care —and some anxiety—the master mason examines the main mass of marble.

8. Squaring the Block

The next day, the large pieces of marble that were cut away from the block are removed so as not to hinder work. The block is still irregular in shape, and the thickness of the remaining superfluous layer varies from place to place. A new stage in the work immediately begins: carving all sides of the block to create a relatively smooth surface.

New, more precise measurements and geometrical estimates are now made. This work is entrusted to two very good craftsmen who came to the quarry only a few months ago, having been highly recommended by a merchant from Paros acquainted with the quarry foreman. The foreman wanted to make up his own mind about the newcomers, so he first assigned them various tasks to test their abilities. Now he is in no doubt as to their professional acumen, having seen the skill with which they handled the tools of their trade.

However, the new arrivals are not well acquainted with the geological peculiarities of Pentelic marble, being far more familiar with marble from the Cyclades. But this is much less of a problem than that presented by the newcomers' character. One of them is rather haughty and aggressive and does not appear to be popular in his new working environment. The other gives the impression of being shy, even though he attempts to inspire respect by stressing at every available opportunity that he is the nephew of the architect who erected the largest temple in the Cyclades. His uncle had transported and positioned the four marble blocks for the temple doorway. "Those monoliths were amazingly heavy, a thousand talents each!" The workers listen carefully, often without being able to hide their admiration—or jealousy. In order to avoid conflicts between the newcomers and the others, the foreman arranges for the newcomers to work by themselves. Their colleagues, however, often approach them with feigned indifference that sometimes fails to hide a deeper curiosity as to what professional "secrets" the newcomers may know.

Their self-confidence clearly discernible, the two craftsmen prepare for work by first making careful measurements. Immediately afterward, they carve channels on the block's upper surface to act as guidelines for further cutting. Then they carve vertical guidelines at the four corners, which will help in leveling the sides and will also establish the exact boundaries for the underside.

9. Overturning the Block to Work on the Underside

Now that the block's upper surface has been prepared and the position of the corners is marked, the block must be turned upside down so rough preparation work can begin on the underside.

After inspecting the block again, the craftsmen use powerful levers to lift it momentarily, placing a few cylindrical iron rollers underneath it to help move it, even though the lower surface's natural anomalies make the rollers less than fully effective. Resistance, at times moderate and at others great, is eventually overcome by the superior power of a few levers and two winches. The block is then dragged to the edge of the parent rock shelf, where the applied force of winches, not to mention the marble's own massive weight, cause it to fall upside down onto the surface below. With a great crash, it lands on top of strong timber beams and a pile of marble chippings, sending clouds of dust into the air. The marble chips cushion the block's fall, and the wooden beams will be used later to help move it laterally.

10. Stages in the Formation of the Column Capital

The future column capital is now much lighter, weighing not more than twenty-five large bulls, and it lies upside down some distance from where it was extracted. Work will proceed to provide it with as perfect a geometric shape as possible. Many stages are involved in a geometric construction: defining the basic reference surface, locating a center and two basic drafted margins, establishing the vertical central axis, and so on.

Rulers, calipers, and various squares and angles are indispensable tools constantly employed in the work of roughly cutting the marble. Removing the excess surface always involves use of the *tykos,* a heavy pick with a long, sharply edged stylet. The *kopeus,* or pointed chisel, is used for carving the drafted margins along which the excess marble will be cut.

The column capitals made for the first marble Parthenon were larger than those made for the newer Parthenon. A half-finished column capital, as transported from the quarry, weighed almost 500 talents (about 12 tons). Of course, the block had weighed much more in its earlier stages, for it had been steadily whittled down from quarrying until the carving of the half-finished shape.

The initial mass of marble for this column capital, which gave so much trouble to the quarry foreman, must have weighed at least 1,600 talents (about 40 tons). If we subtract 500 talents (the weight of the column capital) and 100 to 200 talents (the weight of the large fragments that were initially cut away), that leaves about 900 talents of useless material and chippings. Loosely piled together, the excess marble would take up almost as much space as the original compact block and would weigh about 22 tons.

It took about two months of work in the quarry to extract the block of marble and carve it into a half-finished column capital. Four to five days were spent to create sockets for the original wedges, the same amount of time to make the grooves and other wedge sockets, a few days more to split the block from the parent rock and move it for the first time, another five days to remove the large fragments of excess marble and many other smaller pieces, a few days to move the block here and there, and many more days for the repetitive stages of fashioning the capital itself.

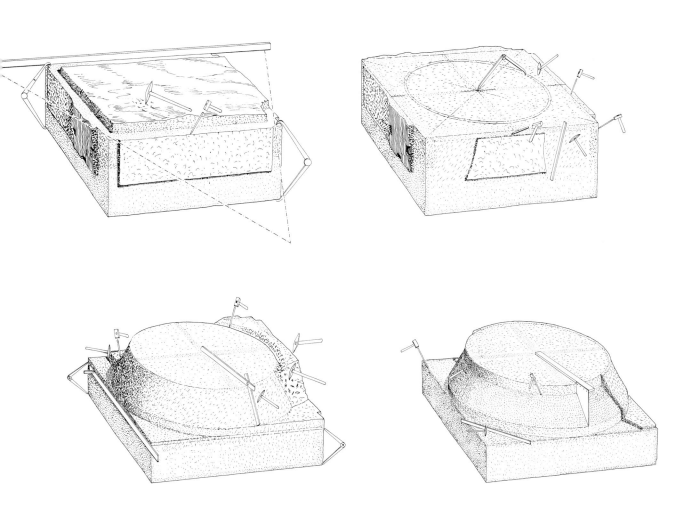

11. Assembling a Timber Sledge

The number of quarrymen needed at any one time depends on the nature of the work to be done. Three to five can accomplish the various tasks involved in cutting sockets. Many more are needed, however, to break the block away from the parent rock, not to mention moving it to and fro afterward, work that demands rope, pulleys, winches, a variety of levers, wooden beams, rollers, and other implements. At last, the day arrives when the half-finished capital is ready to be transported to the Parthenon work site.

Once again, the tireless quarry foreman inspects the stone closely. The marble is impressively pure, as is the quality of the finish. The smile of a contented craftsman begins to play across his lips. But something troubles him, and not for the first time. Almost from the outset, his experienced eye had discerned an extensive fissure passing through the original block. This means the foreman must be extremely careful when he selects the capital's position within the original marble mass. The capital will not fit completely on either side of the fissure, so the crevice will have to run through its center, far from the exposed edges. The foreman believes that, despite its fissure, the capital will be able to support heavy structural loads. His final decision, however, is influenced by the marble's otherwise excellent appearance. After thinking for some time, he orders his workers to prepare the marble for transport.

Early in the morning of the next day, the quarrymen, equipped with extremely strong and massive wooden levers, gradually begin to lift the capital. Bit by bit, they assemble large and small wooden beams underneath it. The sledge they are forming is essential in the first stage of pulling the load from the quarry depths—a task that requires great effort—and then for the relatively simple procedure of moving it down to the base of the mountain.

A number of quarrymen complete a task begun the previous day. They flatten out or remove marble chips and lay long timber planks along the corridor through which the sledge will be hoisted to the quarry entrance. Other quarrymen lay out two long, powerful ropes. They fasten one end of each rope to the sledge. They wrap the other ends in three or four loops around the sturdy wooden axles of two massive winches located slightly further up at the quarry entrance.

Both winches were made by the finest engineers of the day out of extremely sturdy and resilient wood. Being much more powerful than those used in boat building, the winches arouse awe in all who see them in action. But the ropes are also the pride of their makers, known as *kalostrophoi,* or rope weavers. They can withstand both the pull of the winches and the enormous combined weight of wagon and capital.

When everything is ready, the strongest quarrymen take hold of the winch levers and, moving slowly, turn the axles until the rope becomes taut. Then they pause while the very hard cylindrical oak rollers are positioned underneath the sledge and a brake is connected at the rear. The brake stops the sledge from backsliding.

Everyone in the quarry appreciates the value of such detailed preparation. The older hands often tell a story, one of many they never tire of reciting, in which a rope snapped, causing a loaded sledge to suddenly slide backward, crushing and killing a quarryman. This no doubt led to the idea of installing a brake. That tragic accident is very much on the mind of one of the quarrymen—a man entrusted with the task of continually moving the oak rollers from the rear to the front of the sledge—when suddenly the foreman gives the order for work to begin. The great mass of marble finally embarks on its journey.

The powerful winch axles slowly turn three times, creaking encouragingly. Sweat covers the winch operators, who are already breathing rapidly. The sturdy ropes are pulled taut, like the strings of two enormous bows capable of shooting an arrow as big as a tree. Nevertheless, the load remains motionless. The winch operators apply even more force. Suddenly, before the fourth turn is completed, the great load, protesting with spasms and creaks, reluctantly begins to move to the quarry entrance, defeated at last by sheer human determination.

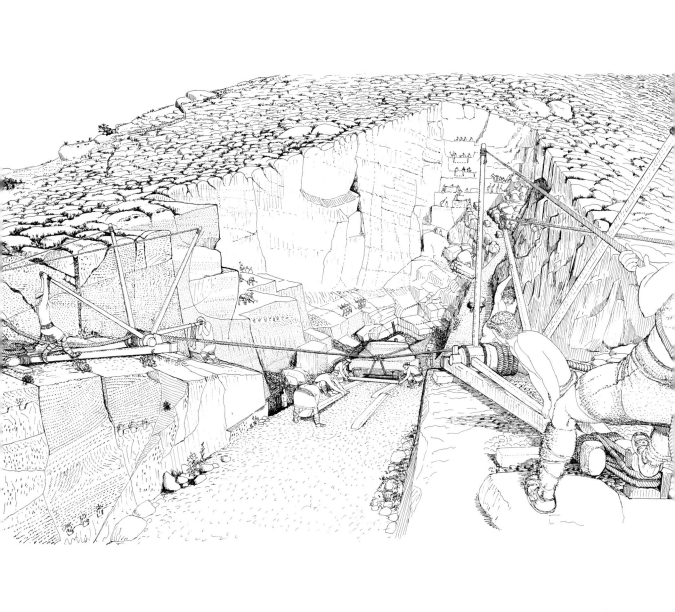

13. Descending to the Loading Platform

Taking turns at the arduous work of operating the winches, the quarrymen have slowly brought the great load to the apex of its ascent. Now the descent toward Athens begins. For tens of millions of years, this mass of marble had rested in the mountain's depths. Now, seeing the light of day and being fashioned by beings more short-lived even than the surrounding shrubs, it bestows something of eternity on mankind.

The load must travel down a narrow and straight, but quite steep, flagstone road to arrive at a loading area, where it will be hoisted onto a wagon. The forces of weight and friction that made the capital's ascent to the quarry mouth so difficult will facilitate its descent to the loading platform. Friction, which keeps the sledge from sliding on the steep flagstone road, is reduced slightly by greasing the flagstones with animal fat, and is no greater than the weight's downward pull. Workers control the capital's descent by using wooden levers to guide the sledge; to reduce acceleration, ropes attached to the sledge are slowly tied and untied around stakes secured at intervals in the ground. By evening of the same day, the half-finished column capital has arrived at the loading platform.

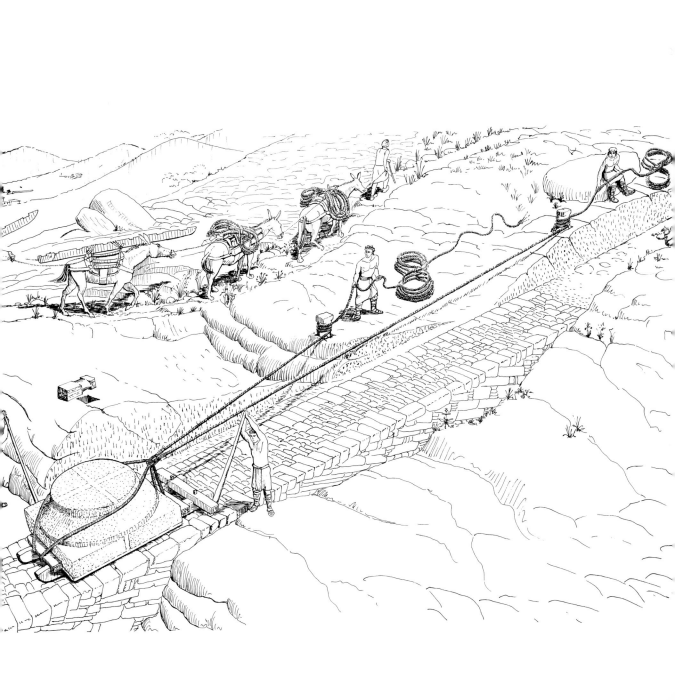

14. Loading the Capital onto the Large Wagon

After reaching the loading platform, the sledge, which is no longer needed here, must be returned to the quarry. The first quarry sledges were probably heavy ones made of a solid piece of wood. Dragging such a sledge back to the quarry would have been a difficult task, requiring many workers, animals, and winches, and doing so would have reduced workers' access to the road. We may suppose, therefore, that the sledge could be dismantled. Its individual components, along with the ropes, could thus have been carried back to the quarry with greater ease, each of them loaded onto a few pack animals driven on paths a little beyond the flagstone road.

These mundane tasks take place a little before sunset, just as another work team undertakes to load the capital onto a large wagon that arrived a few hours earlier. Known as a *tetrakykle,* the heavy wagon is the pride of a renowned wagon builder. It is perhaps the largest and sturdiest ever to have traversed the approximately 94 stades (17 kilometers) from Pentelicon to Athens.[3] It travels just a little slower than the smaller wagons used to transport the blocks of the temple walls. But the *tetrakykle* requires a well-built road that can endure heavy loads; also, it is far from flexible, because many teams of pack animals are needed to draw it. Square and round masses are loaded from the side, while narrow or long blocks are loaded from the back.

Loading the column capital requires relatively little effort, thanks to the specially developed loading platform at the end of the road and the amazing skill of the quarrymen. Two sturdy beams, a few oak rollers, and three or four levers are enough to move the great mass of marble onto the wagon.

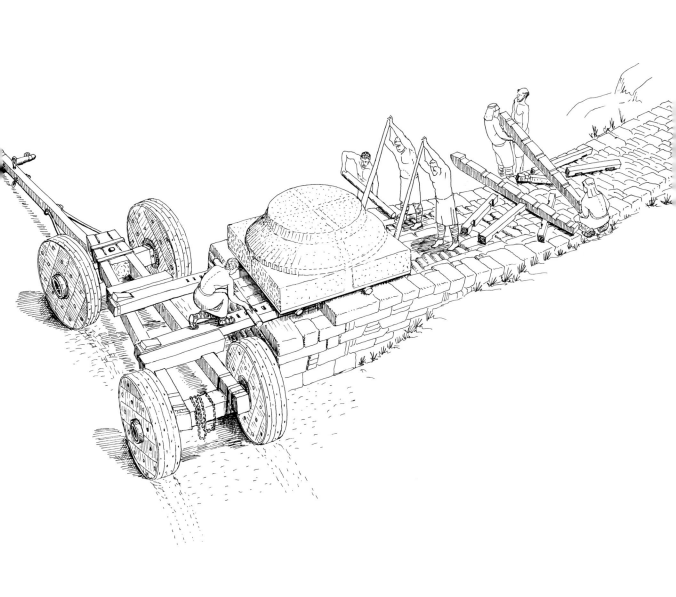

15. On the Road to Athens

The next day, early in the morning, the wagon starts for Athens. The mules are well rested, having been left to graze throughout the afternoon of the previous day. The prospects for the journey, the so-called *lithagogia,* bode well; the driver has inspected the road carefully to be certain that it is in good condition. In general, Athenians transport heavy loads well after the rainy season, when the roads are dry and hard, and when longer days allow journeys to be made without haste. Other possible obstacles and difficulties, often unforeseen, are thus also avoided.

During the summer months, wagonloads of marble coming from the quarry are a regular occurrence. Judging from the amount of marble used for the Parthenon and the short period in which the temple was built, each summer's day would have seen at least fifteen different wagons traveling the road between Mount Pentelicon and Athens.

The wagon that now carries our half-finished capital is perhaps the largest and most impressive one of all. At every point along the way, people leave their daily chores to gaze at the spectacle, some out of simple curiosity, others with awe and admiration; some with uneasiness, still others with skepticism. No one, however, remains indifferent to the mechanical achievement of the wagon builder's art, not to mention the gigantic load of marble it hauls.

Just before midday, as a slope in the road affords steady and almost effortless progress, the hill of Lycabettus looms on the right. The Acropolis, which for most of the journey has been hidden by the pleasant aspect of Lycabettus, now begins to appear in its entirety, together with the rest of the city of Athens. Behind this wonderful landscape shines the blue sea, its colors vying with the often-praised clarity of the Attic sky.

Despite the heat of the midday sun, many farmers stand to admire yet again the *pentelethen lithagogia,* the "conveying of stone from Pentelicon." They are happy, not only because of the splendid building program being executed on the Acropolis, but also because of the good harvest reaped during the last few days and the recent fine crop of well-ripened grapes from the vineyards on the slope of Lycabettus.

16. On the Eastern Outskirts of the City

Some 10 stades (1.85 kilometers) remain before the wagon reaches the Acropolis. Thanks to the careful work of the road builders and the condition of the wagons, animals, and men, the journey has been free of problems. In the past, a collapsed section of road or a split wagon axle could halt traffic for two entire days, costing time and money. Setbacks such as these, however, provided valuable lessons for builders of road and wagon alike.

The road slopes down more steeply, but not enough to necessitate the use of the brake. The driver, the rein-holder, and their assistants (the *zeugetrophoi,* who both prodded and cared for the animals) now cast a melancholy glance to their left at the low but striking bulk of the gigantic, half-finished Temple of Olympian Zeus.[4] From stories told to them by their elders and from their own childhood memories, they know that the huge drums that make up the temple's columns—even larger and heavier than our capital—were brought here more than twenty-five years ago from quarries of the Peiraic coast. It seems unbelievable that blocks weighing 13 tons could be transported over a distance of some 12 kilometers and an ascent of 81 meters above sea level.

17. Passing the South Slope of the Acropolis

The road continues its downward course for 2 stades (370 meters). Now the wagon is within the city and trundles along between the houses of the Athenians. A single stop is made, outside the Shrine of Dionysus Eleuthereus, where fresh mules are harnessed onto those at the front. They are needed because the road begins to rise. It is only 2 1/2 stades up to the great bend, where the mules are unharnessed from the wagon and where the last and most difficult part of the ascent to the Acropolis will begin. The most awkward section of the road for the animals is the distance between the Sanctuary of the Nymph and the great bend, a length measuring some one hundred paces. A plan to reduce the problems encountered here has been worked out. It involves leveling out the small declivity to the south by filling it in with firmly packed material, and building a sturdy retaining wall. The project has constantly been postponed, however, in order to build the many houses in the vicinity.[5] It would finally be implemented at a later time. It is difficult to imagine how the wagon traversed this particular spot in the interim period.

While the wagon passes the south slope of the Acropolis, the driver and his companions ecstatically behold the first courses of the great temple's colonnades rising above them on the crest of the rock. How strange these hetero-geneous shapes appear. On the one hand, there is the simple and austere geometric form of the new temple's foundations; on the other, the winding snakelike body of the ancient wall alternates with the irregular and uneven surface of the exposed rock under and above it. Who ordained that the building program on the rock should continue? Who foresaw what the Acropolis might finally look like? Who had even the slightest idea that new, broader structures would one day be built on the southern slope?

The distance from the great bend to the site of the ancient gate, where a new propylon (marble entrance gate) is also being erected, is only one stade (185 meters), but the gate is more than 40 meters above the bend! Thus, the power needed to drag the capital to its destination is much greater than what twenty beasts of burden could apply. Even four times this number would not suffice to haul this load up such a slope. Furthermore, there is not enough space on the road for so many animals. It is necessary to employ the same mechanisms used earlier to pull the blocks of marble up from the depth of the quarries.

This problem had been overcome about four decades ago, when the architraves and other large blocks were needed for the limestone Temple of Athena (the so-called Archaios Neos) and four decades before that, when similar blocks were hauled up for the first large stone Temple of Athena (the so-called Hekatompedon). The blocks used for the Hekatompedon's large pedimental sculptures extended back into the wall to act as structural supports and at times weighed more than 7 tons. Winches alone could not haul such weights onto the Acropolis, especially if the marble had to be pulled over the irregular surface of the slopes or along serpentine paths. A ramp was essential, and such an inclined surface appears to have been used even centuries earlier, in the Mycenaean period, to transport the great blocks used to build the giant stone wall.

The western approach to the Acropolis consisted of an impressive ramp, 10 meters wide and 80 meters long, built in the Archaic period. Large sections of its retaining wall can still be seen today.[6] Even during the years when the first marble temple was constructed, this approach was already quite ancient and in a way had itself become associated with the shrine's architectural character. Nevertheless, those who knew something of the work undertaken on the Acropolis up to that time realized that the main, if not the only, reason for the ramp's construction was purely practical: to facilitate the ascent of the massive blocks for the Archaic temple. There may have been other reasons of an architectural nature, but they could not have been of fundamental importance.

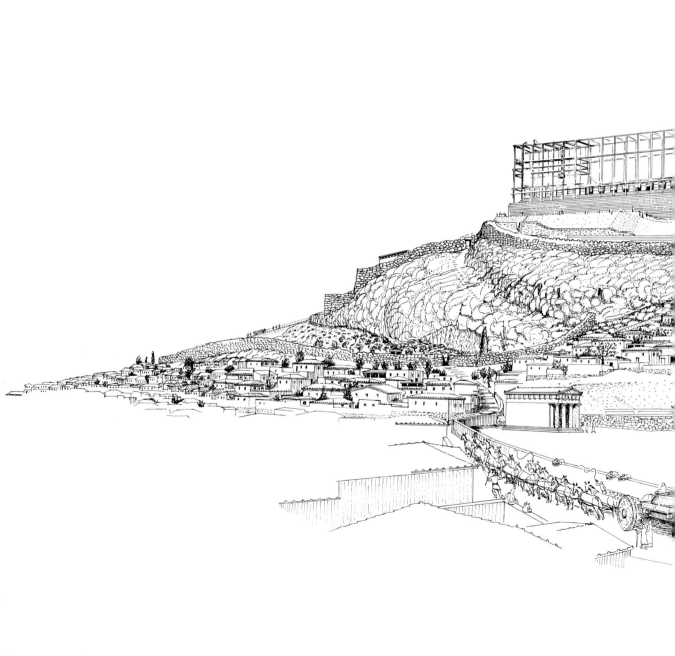

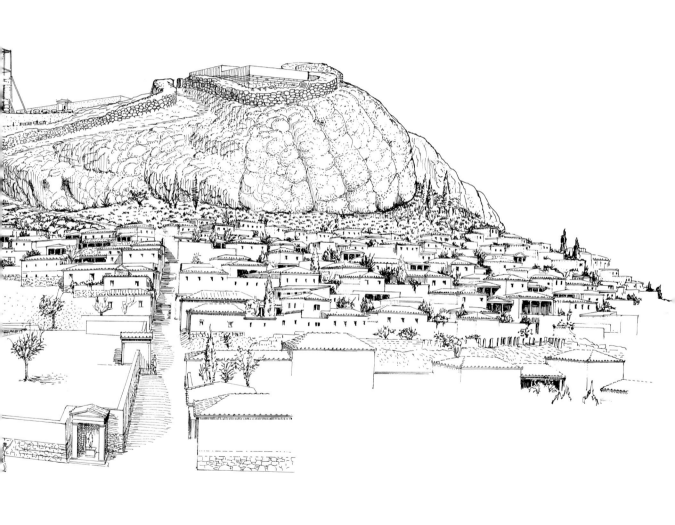

Thoughts such as these must have lingered in the minds of the laborers each time they conveyed marble blocks for the large temple via the tried-and-true ramp.

Long experience in the quarries of Pentelicon and Paros has yielded a store of specialized knowledge about drawing heavy loads on inclined surfaces. Here at the Athenian Acropolis, this knowledge can be utilized as techniques are perfected.

In the quarries, marble blocks are loaded onto sledges; just below the Acropolis, however, they are transferred to wagons, which are much easier and far quicker to pull. There was apparently no other effective way to bring the marble up to the propylon. This method requires, first and foremost, a sound brake system to protect both men and wagon. But here a faster, more efficient traction system is employed than in the quarry depths: we may call it the "balanced wagon" method.

Huge pulleys, flexibly attached by ropes to stakes in the ground, are needed at the upper point of each straight section of the route. That all the ropes have to be particularly strong goes without saying. The balanced wagon system is as simple as it is effective: the force needed to haul a loaded wagon up the ramp is transferred, via the pulley, from a team of mules pulling an empty wagon down the ramp.[7] As each wagon arrives at the top and delivers its load, the mules are harnessed to it. Instead of wasting almost all their strength in ascending the incline, the animals simply have to drag the empty wagon to the bottom, their horse-power being supplemented to a large extent by their own physical weight. This system is highly effective because it turns a disadvantage—the wagon's dead weight—into an advantage. As the animals descend the ramp, their effort is transformed from being futile into being doubly effective. The problem of the confined space at the top of the ramp is eliminated, while at the same time both the ascent of a loaded wagon and the safe descent of an empty one are facilitated.

No doubt the builders of the Parthenon valued this system from the project's very outset, as it ensured that a great deal of marble could be brought up each day. One of our laborers must have turned all this over in his mind before asking his companions:

"How many huge marble blocks do you think have been hauled up here in the five years that they've been building the temple?"

"Pentelic? Or Peiraic as well?" asked the driver.

"Everything, naturally!"

"That's a difficult one, but I'd say about ten to eleven thousand."

"That's my estimate as well. More than ten wagonloads daily, if we leave out the days when rain and mud made transport impossible. But, without our method of balancing the weight of the wagons, we wouldn't have been able to get even half the amount of marble up there, even if we were twice the number of men!"[8]

The men all know that the architects addressed these important mechanical matters when they decided which methods would prove most effective and least time-consuming. They probably do not know, however, exactly how many of the new ideas are indeed the architects', and how many have been borrowed. But the wagon driver is certain of one thing: quite apart from the inspiration of architects and specialists, the main prerequisite for the safe and effective operation of any mechanism is the carefulness, knowledge, and prudence of all those participating in the work. Thus, while waiting to take his wagon up the ramp, he devotes much of his time to inspecting painstakingly not only the wagon parts—especially the pole—but also the machines and pulleys, the ropes and the stakes to which they are attached, and even the ramp's very surface. Finally, he adjusts the distance between the brake and the wheels.

Twenty mules are then harnessed to the empty wagon at the top of the ramp, and its descent begins. The immensely resistant *kalos,* the largest and best rope used here, becomes encouragingly taut and begins to drag the loaded wagon up the ramp. The undertaking must be divided into two stages, for as the ramp ascends it takes a turn to the right. Thus, the wagon must stop for a while.

The second stage of the ascent takes place just like the first, with the ropes being passed through a large pulley secured outside the gates to the Acropolis. Now the excellent organization of the entire operation pays off, and the great column capital stands on the platform in front of the propylon as dusk begins to spread its rosy mantle over the landscape.

The next day, before the stars have even left the morning sky, the massive but now empty wagon sets off once again for the quarry. A stone mason from Naxos claims that this time the wagon would return with the first of the marble blocks for the temple's architrave (the long horizontal portion that rests atop the capitals): "If all goes well, in a few months, when the first column capitals are in place, we can set up the architrave immediately." However, a former companion-in-arms of Callimachus (the military commander of the Battle of Marathon), voices concern about certain developments in far-off lands. "If what is said about Darius's serious illness is true, then no one knows if in ten months we shall be able to continue work on erecting the architrave!"

These troubling thoughts are dispelled by the foreman's salutation. He has come to give instructions about how the capital should be moved to the Parthenon. As in the quarry, the transport system relies on a sledge and oak rollers. This time, though, the sledge moves along a permanent wooden track running from the propylon to the temple. Hauled by two winches, the marble finally arrives at a platform to the east of the Parthenon, just before the Agora (marketplace) opens to fill with the jostling morning crowd. The newly arrived capital joins dozens of half-worked column drums and a few other partly finished column capitals.[9]

Here, skilled stone masons finish only the drums' lower surface. The upper surface is carefully completed by other masons immediately after the drum is set in place. Thus, the columns are erected in the quickest possible way. Because the column capitals must be completely finished before they can be hoisted into position, work begins on them even as the first row of column drums is being installed. Two of the column capitals are already close to completion and begin to take on their final shape. They differ little from those of the most recent limestone temple being of the same size with a slightly lower *echinus* (rounded molding) and a thicker neck. These variations are due mostly to the increased height of the new temple's columns, to the nature of the construction material, and to new architectural concepts.

20. A Dilemma: Greater Economy or Greater Security?

The next day, one of the architects must inspect the newly arrived, half-finished column capital. He has already been informed of the presence of the fissure and must assess the seriousness of the problem. It would seem, however, that he reaches much the same conclusions as the quarry foreman did three days earlier, for he orders carving to proceed and entrusts two of the finest stone masons on the work site with the task.

First, the masons carefully examine the dimensions and the corners of the half-finished capital, work that demands expert knowledge of geometry. Second, they begin to prepare the first drafted margins for carving the capital's resting surface. This enables them to examine the fissure more closely and to estimate the extent of the handicap, especially with regard to carving at those points where the fissure would meet the delicately chiseled lines along the lower portion of the column capital. Then they ask the architect for his professional opinion.

Much discussion ensues. All the evidence seems to indicate that the capital should be set aside and that work should continue on the other column capitals. After new half-finished column capitals have been received, it will be easier to judge the relative quality of our capital with its fissure.

"If, in the end, it is deemed suitable, it must be reinforced with quite a number of hidden iron clamps on both its surfaces," says the architect with a trace of weariness.[10]

"Let us hope that it can be saved!" comes the passionate reply from the oldest of all the craftsmen, while the youngest looks on anxiously. How thrilled the youngster has been over the last few days that he should be included in such an important part of the work. The architect, sensitive to the feelings of the aspiring craftsman, adds a few words of soothing optimism. "There are still quite a few possibilities, so don't give up. Your thirst may yet be quenched." Deep inside, though, he is almost certain that the column capital will be deemed unsuitable. Nevertheless, he ends the discussion by saying, "For the time being, we shall put off a decision and think a little more about the matter." Many days pass and no further work is undertaken on the capital.

This unlucky turn, which seemed so serious at the time, pales in comparison to the misfortunes that soon befall the Athenian state. Unfortunately, King Darius in distant Persia breathes his last, and his successor, Xerxes, younger and more energetic, begins to prepare a new campaign against Greece.

21. The Work Site after the Persian Attack

The governing regime in Athens changes abruptly as a shift in policy is needed to meet the new threat. Themistocles, who now leads the Athenians, cannot afford to indulge in the luxuries of temple building. All the state's efforts are devoted to building ships and preparing a new and strong navy, fortifying the harbor of Piraeus, and manufacturing a sufficient supply of weapons.[11] Therefore, the great building project on the Acropolis grinds to a halt. The brilliant artists, architects, and craftsmen undertake duties of a different kind, but they never lose hope that they will one day continue work on the Acropolis. Forty years will pass before their hopes can materialize.[12] By then, the glorious half-finished temple lies ruined, consumed by the flames of the Persians.

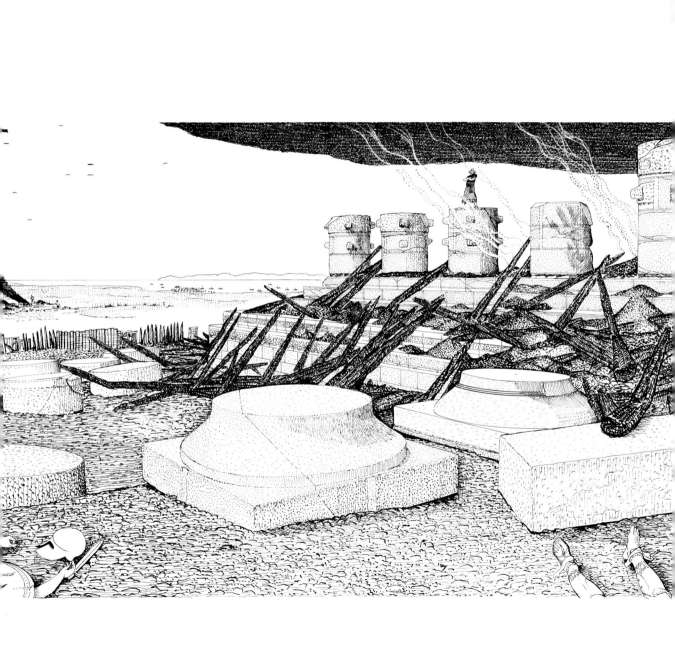

22. The Same Site, Fifty Years Later

One of the craftsmen who had worked on the column capital met a hero's death in the fight against the Persians of 480 B.C. Another, younger member of the work team is now a venerable old man who still practices his wonderful craft. For decades following the great war with the Persians, temple-building programs were postponed, and there were few opportunities for stone masons. Our worthy craftsman, along with his contemporaries, spent the best years of his life engaged in brick making and shipbuilding. Twice more he offered his military services, and on even more occasions he was obliged to serve abroad. But he is lucky to have survived—to see the day when, following the signing of the peace accords some ten years earlier, the state would decide to continue the temple-building program. And so, once again, we find him working on the Acropolis.

For ten years he has toiled with admirable resilience, helping to carve the threshold, the cornices (horizontal moldings), and the capitals of the *antae* (the pilasters—columns placed flush against the wall—at the ends of the projecting walls flanking the entrance to the temple). By a coincidence of fate, he now finds himself at exactly the same spot where he was fifty years ago, when he was just eighteen years old and full of so many dreams. During his last, fleeting days at the work site, he sometimes finds himself lost in thought, reminiscing about the past. Just today, in fact, while lifting his gaze to the pediment, he caught sight of the column capitals, and for a

moment tears welled in his eyes. But life, as always, continues. The Parthenon, the most illustrious building ever erected by the state, and the greatest accomplishment in the technology of stone, is almost finished.

The ambitious building program spearheaded by the Athenian leader Pericles has no precedent. Each of the old buildings is to be rebuilt, and the surface area is to be almost completely transformed. Both architects and sculptors think in new ways. Almost nothing has remained of the plans for the first marble temple; only the diameter of the columns is the same.[13] Although the columns are even taller than those initially planned,[14] their capitals are clearly smaller. Indeed, a few of these have been carved from the older capitals. Our veteran mason is one of the very few people who knows which of the forty-six column capitals of the colonnade have been fashioned out of the handful of older, half-finished capitals. He is also aware that the capital with the fissure was never used, even though he cannot locate it now. He thought he saw it used as a pedestal, but cannot remember exactly where.[15] "That's what time has in store for us all," he murmurs with a degree of melancholy every time his thoughts return to wars and work.

23. Time Future

The adventures of the half-worked column capital continued during the centuries that followed, and they continue to this day. But the capital's story will remain incomplete, just like the marble itself, for we cannot journey back to that brilliant epoch to walk among the ancients. Almost twenty-five hundred years have passed and a hundred generations have come and gone since the last appearance of our column capital. Ensuing generations could never even contemplate having the luxury of modern scientific curiosity; the struggle for survival occupied their waking hours. History was recorded only rarely, and often with distortions; generations relied on oral traditions to pass on their legacy.

For centuries afterward, Athens was little more than a village, a fraction of its ancient size, with dwellings that resembled huts more than houses. Workers no longer traversed great distances between quarries and building sites, for the ancient monuments themselves had become quarries. Later generations managed to transform one hundred thousand tons of sculpture and hewn marble, which had once belonged to the buildings of antiquity, into ten million shapeless pieces, collectively worth a million times less than the works destroyed to produce them. Imagine cutting the *Mona Lisa* into strips to make soles for the shoes of the blind.

On the Acropolis, all the ancillary buildings and thousands of small monuments were destroyed. Only a skeleton now remains of the Parthenon. Excavations in the last century uncovered innumerable fragments of stone statues—but nothing in bronze, which would have been a more popular and important material. Then there are the hundreds of fractured inscriptions, thousands of sherds, and the foundations of some smaller structures. Tens of thousands of smaller marble fragments have also been found, originating not only from the Acropolis but also from buildings all over Athens. One of the hundreds of larger fractured blocks from the Acropolis monuments now lies some 40 meters east of the Erechtheum. It is all that remains of the block of marble profiled in this book. At some point, that block was split into two along the length of its fissure. Only the smaller part survives today. The bottom of the capital and all its edges and corners were destroyed at a later date when large chunks were cut away, possibly to procure small pieces for building purposes. The flat side seems at some stage to have been used as a threshold.[16] But this, together with its fate in antiquity after its rejection, must remain the stuff of conjecture.

"That's what time has in store for us all," one might say with a degree of melancholy.

1. Pre-Parthenon, Older Parthenon, Elder Parthenon, Parthenon II, and so on are the conventional names used from the beginning of the nineteenth century onward for the marble temple that preceded the Parthenon. The half-worked drums of this building, visible on the north wall of the Acropolis, where they have been reused, were recognized and studied for the first time (1806) by W. M. Leake. In 1835 Ludwig Ross determined that the foundations and the solid base of the Parthenon belonged to the older temple.

2. On the size and shape of the levers we have only scanty indications.

3. The ancient stade equaled 600 feet and differed from place to place. In Olympia, it was 192.27 meters, while in Athens 185 meters.

4. It was not possible for the work of many teams of animals to be controlled by the driver alone. The *zeugetrophoi* had to accompany the animals on foot to force them to work, the mules with a whip and the oxen with a goad. The *zeugetrophoi* also made sure that the animals were well cared for.

5. The remains of houses behind the sturdy retaining wall south of the Herodeion have been dated to the middle of the fifth century B.C.

6. J. Travlos, *Pictorial Dictionary of Ancient Athens* (London, 1971), figs. 608, 609.

7. The traction animals are capable of hauling a load even on a downward slope. Suffice it to note that sloping fields may at times be ploughed with mules or horses from upper to lower levels.

8. Until 1940, the largest blocks of marble for the restoration works were lifted onto the Acropolis using an iron wagon moving on iron rails, and pulled from the Propylaea by a hand-operated iron winch. Work was tiresome and time consuming. However, the 1986 ascent of a new, 13.5-ton marble block at the southeast corner of the Acropolis using a powerful electric crane, and the block's subsequent move by rail to the Parthenon, was a very difficult and time-consuming task lasting five hours and demanding the labor of an average of ten people.

9. Twelve half-finished column drums were uncovered on the open-air work site excavated in 1835. A few implements were found among these column drums, along with vases containing fine red ochre used as a coloring agent by the stone masons.

10. In antiquity, clamps were used to reinforce architectural members in the places of natural fissures or cracks. Such reinforcements have been observed on the upper surface of the capital of the seventh column of the Parthenon's east colonnade during structural restoration work in 1990. These reinforcements provide an idea of the manner in which the half-finished column capital may have been reinforced.

11. Herodotus 7.144; Thucydides 1.14.2 and 93.4.

12. Work on the Parthenon began again in 447 B.C.—when Pericles was leader of the Athenians—with the dismantling of a section of a part of the Older Parthenon and the transport of blocks from Piraeus for widening the foundation by almost five meters and a corresponding widening of the stepped base. In 440 B.C., the temple was roofed, and in 438 it was completed, including the colossal gold-and-ivory statue of Athena Parthenos.

13. 1.91 meters, but the shape of the fluting in cross-

Notes

section changes from being simply round earlier to false-elliptical now.

14. Approximately 10.43 meters instead of approximately 9.55 meters.

15. At the lower part of the capital is part of a large rectangular cutting with restored dimensions: 87 centimeters long, 40 centimeters wide, and 50 centimeters or more deep, which in all probability points to the capital's secondary use: placed upside down as a heavy base for a large wooden post.

16. In 1990, using powerful machines, the block was moved and positioned on a small base, which made its flat, upper surface visible.

Glossary

Cross-references in the glossary appear in boldface type.

Acropolis Greek for "high city." The Acropolis of **Athens** is the tall rock outcrop, immediately south of the ancient town of Athens, where an assemblage of temples was constructed, notably the Temple of Athena Parthenos, the city goddess of Athens. The word "acropolis" is used also for the highest part of other ancient Greek towns, which was often fortified.

Agora In ancient Greek towns, a public market and meeting place that formed the center of civic life, where merchants had their stalls and business was transacted. The Athenian Agora was at the base of the northern slope of the **Acropolis**.

Archaic period The period in ancient Greece from 750 to 480 B.C.

architrave In classical architecture, the lowest part of the **entablature**: the horizontal beam that rests directly on top of the column **capitals**.

Athens The capital of modern Greece. Athens was one of the leading cities of ancient Greece and the capital of the city-state by the same name.

Battle of Marathon An epic battle in which Athenians defeated the Persians; fought in 490 B.C. on the plain of Marathon, 42.2 kilometers north of the city of **Athens**. The modern Marathon race replicates the distance traveled by the ancient runner who brought news of the victory to the city of Athens. *See also* **Persia**.

Callimachus Commander-in-chief of the Athenians at the **Battle of Marathon**. He died in that battle.

capital The top part of a column, between the shaft of the column itself and the overlying horizontal **architrave**. Three **orders** of columns were used in antiquity.

column drum A cylindrical section of the shaft of an ancient column. Drums were stacked one atop another to form the finished column shaft.

cornice The uppermost part of the **entablature** of a classical building. It is made up of a series of projecting horizontal moldings.

Cyclades A group of islands in the Aegean Sea, southeast of **Athens**. The islands form a circle (Greek *kyklos*, hence the name of the island group) around the central island of Delos. Among the most important of the Cycladic islands are **Naxos**, **Paros**, and **Delos**.

Darius King of the Persians from 522 to 486 B.C. It was his army that was defeated by the Greeks in the **Battle of Marathon** in 490 B.C. *See also* **Persia**.

Delos The small central island in the **Cyclades**.

Delphi One of the holiest sites of ancient Greece. Located northwest of

Glossary

Athens, Delphi was considered the center of the world. It was the seat of the Delphic oracle and a place sacred to the worship of Apollo and other gods.

Doric order   The style of column **capitals** used in the **Parthenon**. *See also* **orders**.

echinus   The convex molding that forms the lower part of a Doric column **capital**.

entablature   The horizontal part of a classical building that rests on the tops of the column **capitals**. From top to bottom, the entablature consists of three parts: **cornice**, **frieze**, and **architrave**.

Erechtheum   Smaller temple on the **Acropolis** of **Athens** dedicated to several cult figures. It was built shortly after the **Parthenon**.

frieze   The central part of the **entablature** of a classical building.

Hymettus   One-thousand-meter high mountain ridge east of **Athens** where much of the marble used for construction in ancient Athens was quarried.

Ionia   Western Asia Minor, that is, the west coast of present-day Turkey and some of the islands off the coast.

Ionic order   One of the three **orders** of columns and **capitals** used in antiquity.

lithagogia   Greek for "conveyance of stones." It refers to the transfer of stones from the quarry to the building site.

Lycabettus   Almost 300-meter-tall mountain northeast of the ancient city of **Athens**. Today it lies within the city limits.

Mycenaean period   The period of the Bronze Age, from 1575 to 1050 B.C., when the city of Mycenae in northeastern Peloponnesus flourished. Mycenae was the capital of King Agamemnon, one of the leaders of the Trojan War.

Naxos   The largest of the islands of the **Cyclades**. It was seized by the Persians in 490 B.C. but came under the rule of Athens in 471 B.C.

order   A style of column and **capital**. The three orders used in classical architecture are **Ionic**, **Doric** (the style used for the **Parthenon**), and Corinthian.

Paros   One of the islands of the **Cyclades**. The island is formed by a 700-meter-tall mountain, whose fine (Parian) marble was quarried in antiquity and widely used by sculptors.

Parthenon   The main temple on the Athenian **Acropolis**, dedicated to the city's patron goddess, Athena. The Parthenon, whose ruins still rise spectacularly atop the Acropolis, was the last of a number of successive temples to the goddess on the Acropolis.

pediment   The triangular gable on the short side of a building with a pitched roof. In classical architecture, the pediment of a temple was usually decorated with sculptures, as on the **Parthenon**.

pedimental   Of the **pediment**.

Peiraic limestone   Limestone from the coast near **Piraeus**.

Pentelic marble   Marble from Mount **Pentelicon**.

Pentelicon   Mount Pentelicon; 17 kilometers northeast of the city of **Athens**. The marble for the construction of the **Parthenon** was quarried from the 1,100-meter-tall mountain.

Pericles   Ruler of **Athens** from about 460 to 429 B.C. His efforts to make Athens the leading city of Greece included the construction of the **Parthenon** and the **Propylaea** on the **Acropolis**.

Persia   Ancient Iranian empire in southwest Asia. Starting in 550 B.C., the kings of Persia fought a number of wars to expand their realm. Their two attempts to conquer mainland Greece, in 490 and 480/479 B.C., however, were unsuccessful.

Piraeus   The harbor of **Athens**, on the coast 8 kilometers southwest of the city.

Pisistratus   Ruler of **Athens** from 546 to 527 B.C. He promoted the cult of Athena and built a number of temples and shrines in the city.

Propylaea   The entrance building to the **Acropolis** of **Athens** that was constructed during the rule of **Pericles** as part of his program to rebuild the monuments on the Acropolis.

propylon   Large roofed entrance gate.

scission   Split or cut (in marble or stone).

sherd   Fragment of pottery from a broken clay vessel.

Shrine of Dionysus Eleuthereus   Sanctuary on the south side of the Athenian **Acropolis** dedicated to Dionysus, the Greek god of wine. It included a cult statue of the god brought there from Eleuthera in Boeotia, north of **Athens**.

sima **tiles**   Protective tiles used as facing on the eaves of a pitched roof along the long sides of a building as well as along the cornice of the pediment.

stade   Ancient measure of distance. Its length varied from one place to another. In **Athens** it was about 185 meters.

talent   Ancient unit of weight equal to 26 kilograms.

Temple of Athena   The **Parthenon**.

temples of Athena   The succession of temples on the Athenian **Acropolis** that preceded the **Parthenon**.

Temple of Olympian Zeus   Enormous temple northeast of the ancient city of **Athens**. Construction began around 515 B.C. but was abandoned a few years later. The temple was finally completed by the Roman emperor Hadrian in A.D. 131–132. The ruins of the temple are still visible today.

Glossary

Themistocles Athenian statesman who, recognizing the continued threat of the Persians, started the construction of the Athenian harbor at **Piraeus** in the 480s B.C. as well as a program to increase the Athenian fleet.

winch Machine used for pulling or hauling heavy loads. A winch consists of a rope coiled around one or more drums.

Xerxes I Son of **Darius** I, Xerxes I was king of the Persians from 486 to 465 B.C. Unlike his father, Xerxes defeated the Greeks at Thermopylae in 480 B.C. and went on to burn the city of **Athens**. *See also* **Persia**.

Select Bibliography

Γ. Αλευρά-Κοκκορού. "Τα αρχαία λατομεία της Νάξου." *Αρχαιολογική Εφημερίς* 1992.

D. Arnold. *Building in Egypt.* Oxford, 1991.

N. Asgari. "Roman and Early Byzantine Marble Quarries of Proconnesos." 10th International Congress of Classical Archaeology. Ankara-Ismir, 1973 (Ankara, 1978), pp. 467–80.

J. A. Bundgaard. *The Excavation of the Athenian Acropolis.* Copenhagen, 1974.

A. Burford. *The Greek Temple Builders at Epidauros.* Liverpool, 1969.

——— "Heavy Transport in Classical Greece." *The Economic History Review* 13 (1960): 1–18.

J. J. Coulton. *Greek Architects at Work.* London, 1977.

W. B. Dinsmoor. *The Architecture of Ancient Greece.* 3rd ed. London, 1950.

E. Dolci. *Carrara, cave antiche.* Carrara 1980, Viareggio 1981.

J. Durm. *Die Baukunst der Griechen³.* Leipzig, 1910.

A. Dworakowska. *Quarries in Ancient Greece.* Wroclaw, 1975.

J. Clayton Fant. *Cavum Antrum Phrygiae, The organization and Operations of the Roman Imperial Marble Quarries in Phrygia.* Oxford, 1989.

——— "Ideology, Gift and Trade: A Distribution Model for the Roman Imperial Marbles." In *The Inscribed Economy,* edited by W. V. Harris, pp. 145–70. Ann Arbor, Mich., 1993.

B. H. Hill. "The older Parthenon." *American Journal of Archaelogy* 16 (1912): 556.

M. Korres. "The Geological Factor in Ancient Greek Architecture." In *The Engineering Geology of Ancient Works, Monuments and Historical Sites,* edited by P. G. Marinos and G. C. Koukis, pp. 1779–93. Rotterdam, 1988.

M. K. Langdon. "Hymettiana II: An Ancient Quarry on Mt. Hymettos." *American Journal of Archaelogy* 92 (1988): 75–83.

L. and T. Mannoni. *Marble: The History of a Culture.* New York, 1985.

J. B. Ward Perkins. "Marble in Antiquity (Collected Papers)." *Archaeological Monographs of the British School at Rome* 6 (London, 1992).

Plutarch. *Pericles.*

J. H. Randall, Jr. "The Erechtheum Workmen." *American Journal of Archaelogy* 57 (1953): 199–209.

Sodini-Lambraki-Kozelj. "Les Carrières de marbre d'Aliki à l'époque paléochrétienne." *Études Thasiennes* 9 (Paris 1980): 81-143.

L. Tarr. *The History of the Carriage.* New York, 1969.

M. Waelkens, N. Herz, and L. Moens, eds. *Ancient Stones, Quarrying, Trade and Provenance.* Leuven, 1992.

J. Wiseman. "An Unfinished Colossus on Mt. Penteli." *American Journal of Archaelogy* 72 (1968): 75–76.